Coaching at Seventy Miles Per Hour

by Dean H. Morehouse

COACHING AT SEVENTY MILES PER HOUR

and

Trying to Stay in the "Right Lane"

An Experienced Look at Seven Aspects of Coaching

First Edition

DEAN H. MOREHOUSE

HENRY QUILL PRESS
Fremont, Michgan

All rights reserved. No part of this book may be reproduced or transmitted in any form by any means, electronic or mechanical, including photo- copying, recording, or by any storage and retrieval system, without permission in writing from the publisher.

Published by Henry Quill Press

Copyright © 2010 by Dean H. Morehouse

Coaching at Seventy Miles Per Hour:
an experienced look at seven aspects of coaching
Dean H. Morehouse.

-1st edition-

Fremont, Michigan: Henry
    Quill Press, ©2010.

ISBN: 1- 883960- 46- 0

"Illustrations by Jane Stroschin"
Interior and cover design by Jane Stroschin
    www.lakeview73@comcast.net

Printed in the United States of American

FOREWARD

Coaching obviously presents many challenges. This book addresses seven aspects of coaching as seen from my perspective of forty-five plus years of junior high, high school and college athletic coaching.

The intent of the book is to share my coaching experiences. Veteran coaches of all sports may be reminded of times when they were confronted with similar circumstances and remember how they dealt with them. Coaches new to athletic coaching will hopefully take away idea's that will assist them as they develop their own programs.

Coaching is not only applicable to athletics. The director of a play and the orchestra conductor lead (coach) their actors and musicians. Each endeavor we are involved in benefits from coaching. Teaching a child to ride a bike or scientists sharing empirical data both involve coaching.

I recently received an internet communication announcing an audio conference called "Coaching and Mentoring Employees: How to unlock potential, enhance loyalty, and boost productivity". This is a goal for all leaders. The tools needed to put this in to practice are the challenge. Each leader/coach will find techniques that are right for them and their situation.

I also read where a company held sessions called "Coach the Coach". The purpose of these meetings was to get feed back and ideas from their staff about the leadership of the company. It is good to have open lines of communication and seek the input of others.

The leader/coach will need to make decisions and use the information to move the group forward in the best and most positive way.

WE ALL COACH. We may refer to it as mentoring, assisting, helping or sharing but they are all efforts to make one another better at something. Whether you are "coaching" an individual, a group, or an athletic team, the same principals apply.

Everyone sees things differently from their perspective or lens. I see things most times from my athletic lens. Athletic coaches will easily relate to the text and I hope others will translate the theme to their lenses as well.

Enjoy coaching and being coached. Both are important.

Coach

ACKNOWLEDGEMENTS

*Many thanks to **my** coaches.*
What a starting lineup!

- *The Glue*
  Howard and Fredreka (Freddie) Morehouse

My parents made it possible for me to have numerous opportunities as a young person. They inspired, supported and challenged me in all my activities. They encouraged me to have interests in our church, sports, music and acting. Finally, they were wonderful examples of faith, discipline and taught me to have a work ethic.

- *The Point Guard*
  Coach Vern Norris

Mr. Norris was my junior high basketball coach. He became my role model and friend. He was a teacher and coach in the Rockford Public Schools in Rockford, Michigan. He later became the Executive Director of the Michigan High School Athletic Association. The impressions he left with me as an eighth grader are still with me today.

- *The Man in the Middle*
  John Mooy

John and I have been friends since childhood. Our mothers taught school together in Cedar Springs, Michigan and our families have stayed close. John became a teacher and we taught together in Fremont, Michigan. He is a nationally known author, storyteller and sculptor. John and I have collaborated on a number of projects; most of which have landed us in trouble. John also did the voice on the CD for this book.

- *The Finisher*
  Jane Stroschin

Jane is nationally known as an artist, author and illustrator of many children's books. She also is a well known public speaker who gives of her time with a true servant's heart. Jane's knowledge and support were instrumental in this project. Jane designed the cover and did all the art work for the book. Her friendship over the years will always be appreciated.

- *The Ultimate Role Player*
  Lauren Jensen

Lauren first became a friend while playing on the varsity basketball team at Hope College. She was the ultimate team player and example of doing what was best for the team. She is currently teaching and studying at Virginia Tech University in Virginia. She is also a wonderful writer and poet. Lauren introduced me to the "Athletic Lens" concept and encouraged me to write about my coaching experiences.

- *The Assist Leader*
  Marianne Mansfield

Marianne was very valuable as the initial editor of the manuscript. When the project began, it was not clear what the outcome would be. Marianne put clarity to a very rough beginning and made it better. She is a former educator, school administrator and a novelist.

DEDICATION

This book is dedicated to my parents Howard and Fredreka (Freddie) Morehouse. Their guidance and example gave me opportunities to learn from their parenting, to have a work ethic, to always treat others with respect and to try and stay in the "right lane".

and

It is also dedicated to my eighth grade basketball coach Mr. Vern Norris. Coach Norris is the reason I became a coach and is my role model and friend. His example of teaching athletic skills and life skills together is something I have tried to emulate and incorporate in my coaching.

Coaching at Seventy Miles Per Hour

and

Trying to Stay in the "Right Lane"

TABLE OF CONTENTS

Chapter 1............Academics First..........Page 23

Chapter 2............An Art Form..............Page 27

Chapter 3............Balance...................Page 33

Chapter 4............Chemistry................Page 41

Chapter 5............Perspective...............Page 49

Chapter 6............Good Stress...............Page 67

Chapter 7............Personal Rewards........Page 73

About the Author......................Page 81

Introduction

Coaching is a great profession. I love it. It is exhilarating. It is my passion.

I admit coaching hasn't always been fun in every respect, but nothing I have done has had zero negatives. As they say, every job has its positives and negatives. For me, the positives outweigh the negatives 100 to 1 in coaching. I had to experience many rough times before I gained my balance and was able to keep things in perspective. Although I have always been comfortable with people, I had to learn how to build chemistry within the many relationships that are in a coach's life.

To say I enjoy "working" with people is an understatement. I enjoy the gratification received when I am able to help others be better than they thought they could be. When I am unable to help someone achieve success, I feel I haven't done my best. I understand that everyone does not want to get in the carriage I may be driving but it still hurts when I can't help someone move forward.

Many years ago, as a college student, I was

hitchhiking home from Michigan State University (it was safer to do then) and an eighteen-wheeler picked me up. The driver was a great person to talk with and in our conversation he asked me what I was going to be when I grew up. I answered that I wanted to be a coach. I have never forgotten his next question: "Why would you want to put your job and future in the hands of some sixteen-year-old kid?" I was in my counselor's office first thing the next Monday morning at MSU thinking about changing my major.

Obviously I did not change my history major/physical education minor and continued on the path following my mother as a teacher and my dream of one day being a coach. It was the best decision I ever made. It became my life.

Eventually I realized what I was called to do was not about me at all. It was about the path set before me. I had been given a tremendous opportunity and challenge to make a difference in many people's lives. Initially I thought I was only affecting the players, and then I realized it was much more.

I read a study about the relationship between the success of a school's athletic teams and the overall behavior of the student body. There was a direct positive correlation in student grades, school pride, and student behavior when athletic teams were successful. It even affected the community's pride.

The awards and rewards I have received from

being a coach are mentioned throughout this book. The awards are not as meaningful as the rewards. Awards are hung on the wall but rewards—like relationships, friends, the chemistry of a team having success, one-time encounters with fans from other cities, the custodians, the players, the parent thank-you, the play that worked, the scouting, the film work and many other things too numerous to mention—are what makes coaching so special.

After forty-five years of coaching various levels of most team sports, my colleagues and friends have convinced me to share my philosophy of trying to stay in the right lane.

I hope you enjoy it.

It is not good enough for a coach to look at the eligibility list to see who is and who is not eligible.

Chapter 1
Academics First

Although this chapter is the shortest one, its message is the most important: the highest priority is to educate your players. Regardless of the age or gender of your team, as a coach your responsibility is to hold all players accountable for their education.

It is not good enough for a coach to look at the eligibility list to see who is and who is not eligible.

Student athletes must know they are responsible for their actions in the classroom—just as they are accountable for their behavior on the playing field. As a coach, you are a huge part of this process.

Let's assume a student tries out for your team. The action in itself shows that this student has an interest in being a part of something. The student has made a choice to join a team. As the coach, you automatically become partially accountable for the student's success or failure. The other people in the equation are: parents, teachers, peers, and the administration. All of these people are important to a student athlete's success.

The academic standard for players will be

dictated by school policy, which is the measuring stick for eligibility. A coach, however, can encourage his players to go above and beyond the school guidelines. This strategy sends the message to your players to perform at a high level—both in the classroom and on the playing field.

The team goal might be to have all players on the honor roll. Players could mentor each other in subjects that are difficult for one another. Team pride and instilling the importance of doing your best at all times are motivating reasons for establishing this goal.

If a member of the team is sidelined because he is not making the grade in a subject, look to the geese for guidance (see chapter 4). Assign two other players to assist that team member until he is performing well enough grade-wise to re-join the team.

Four years flies by quickly, regardless if it is in high school or college. As an athletic coach you have many individuals to monitor. High school students sometimes don't realize they are preparing themselves for life. College students also struggle with determining a major. They may not know what they want to do as a vocation, but learning life skills is the basis for success. Life skills can be taught at all levels, in a variety of ways, and by numerous people—including athletic coaches.

It takes a dedicated leader and coach to make

a difference in the life of a student. If you do not hold yourself accountable for a student athlete's success, you are not doing the total job of being a coach. Successful coaching is more than acquiring the most wins.

Success on the court and the playing field can be increased by building an academic relationship with your students. They want to be part of what you are in charge of and you can be the difference maker. A good academic relationship with your team members leads to mutual trust, great communication, honesty, loyalty, and friendship—all of which transfers to the on-court relationship.

I know a coach who keeps an "Academic Book" in his office. Every player on the team is responsible for writing the grades they receive on tests, papers, and other assignments in this Academic Book. They must also record their class attendance. The coach monitors this book on a weekly basis and he will check personally with players on their academic progress. A call to a teacher to verify how well a player is doing sends an important message. Players respond well when they get a pat on the back or are offered assistance if needed.

Academic success does not guarantee athletic success; however, it is more rewarding to hold your players accountable for their academics than to have a list of ineligible players.

The highest priority is to educate.

Coaches do not have to win every game to be successful in winning relationships.

Chapter 2
An Art Form

Art seeks to communicate ideas, create a sense of flow and beauty, and stimulate emotions. Coaching, as done by an orchestra conductor, a playwright, a movie director, and an athletic coach, meets the above criteria. Regardless of the instrument held—a baton, a pen, a camera, or a whistle—they are coaches in the true sense of the word

All of these coaches have a vision of what they want to portray and how they will achieve their goal. The final product will be a culmination of their coaching skills and how well they can bring together the various parts (color, movement, and words).

For there to be a successful outcome, a coach needs to have someone to guide and instruct who is willing to learn. It takes a special person to be a successful athletic coach, just like it takes a special person to be a truck driver, a doctor, a nurse, a teacher, a farmer, or any other professional.

Coaching can be stressful but it isn't any more stressful for the "right" person than any other vocation is for someone else. A willing learner and a good coach usually attain their goal.

People coach to help bring things together, like the various actors in a play or the instruments in a symphony orchestra. The leader (coach) conducts, choreographs, and demonstrates. The group practices, with the coach as the leader, until the finished product is attained.

Coaches act as conduits for the people with whom they work. If trust exists between them, a successful coach can lead others where they want to go. Without a trusting relationship, however, there will be little or no movement; there will be no satisfaction attained without the complete trust and cooperation of everyone.

People coach because they get personal satisfaction from leading others to succeed in achieving a common goal. A coach's leadership, like the director of a play or the conductor of an orchestra, is essential to achieving a successful outcome.

Coaching is not easy. You must be a good listener, trustworthy, and able to take criticism from those who don't agree with your leadership—sounds like parenting! (Dad, I can peddle the bike myself!) Coaches need to be able to motivate others and to form and maintain good relationships with the people they are leading.

Coaching is rewarding. The conductor is satisfied when the orchestra plays perfectly. The director of a play feels complete when the audience applauds as the curtain goes down. A parent feels a sense of pride when her child rides a two-wheeler by himself.

The athletic coach feels a sense of accomplishment when the team plays well.

Coaching is demanding upon your time. Trying to attain perfection, or close to it, does not come with one practice session. It takes many hours, from all of the participants, to succeed.

Coaches learn a lot about relationships. They know their success requires the help of many people—players, parents, fellow coaches, media personnel, fans, and support staff. Leaders of extra curricular activities and athletic teams need assistance to be successful. Assistant coaches, orchestra band parents and spouses help in numerous ways. A leader should be very thankful if these people are involved in their programs.

I know of many times when a team dinner was prepared by a coach's spouse, team parents or a team supporter; a bed and meal was given to a player having family issues; used basketball shoes and socks were provided to a player without; a player was given a part time job so they could attend team camp; car washes and bake good sales were organized; and many other helpful actions were done to help a coach. Understanding and supportive people can help make the chemistry of a program better and contribute to its overall success.

Coaches learn something from each one of these relationships. These people are an integral part of any coach's success. Many times they become close friends and confidants. They are great listeners and very supportive. They understand the time involved, appreciate the coach's attention, and they share the opportunity and challenge to make a difference.

For the most part, everyone wants the final product to be a success. Parents are usually supportive of their children and a coach with the attributes listed earlier can engage parents to be part of a bigger picture. Everyone must work together to create a sense of beauty and stimulate emotions. The coach is the key but all others must do their parts.

Coaches who coach for a long time can touch thousands of lives. They have associations with players, parents, fans, school personnel, and entire communities. If they are successful (not just in winning games) they will impact ninety-five percent of these relationships in a positive way.

Coaches do not have to win every game to be successful in winning relationships.

The impact you have on a person might not be realized until many years have passed. A coach may never be thanked for her impact. However, a successful coach knows that she tried.

Inside every good coach is a musician. There

is a rhythm to athletic competitions. Timing and coordination are required of players. Every bounce of a basketball and every squeak of a shoe on a gymnasium floor have a beat and a meaning. Every turnover is like forgotten dialogue in a play or a wrong note coming from an instrument.

Leonard Bernstein, the noted conductor and composer of classical music, was asked "What's the most difficult instrument to play?" He replied, "Second violin. I can get plenty of first violinists, but to find the one who plays second violin with as much enthusiasm…now that's a problem."

Inspire your players to appreciate the art of the sport.

Coaching is about balance. It is about holding yourself accountable to that balance in order to be successful.

Chapter 3
Balance

Like most coaches, I was forced to learn how to juggle, prioritize, multi-task, and balance things early in my career, especially when I was coaching three sports, teaching six classes a day, and driving the team bus.

Balance in coaching takes on a huge array of issues. There is the obvious balance between coach and player. On one hand, the coach is the teacher, instructor, leader, mentor, and the person that holds the player accountable. On the other hand, the coach can be a friend, confidant, and consultant to players.

Then, you need to consider parents; employers; boosters; colleagues; and, most importantly, your family. Balancing all of these people in your life is a lot more difficult than walking on a balance beam! Who is the top priority? You? A particular player? The team? Your employer? Or your family? Obviously, prioritizing circumstances is different for each coach.

I read about a college coach in a very high-profile program who had been fired. At a press conference, the new coach spoke of himself as a "gatherer," someone who would do everything he could to involve the community in his program, be there for players, and be available to the fans and media. After the press conference, a reporter talked about how the former coach had lived on his own island all by himself. According to the reporter, the former coach had not built a foundation that included all the needed pieces to be successful; he was an isolationist not a gatherer.

    The balance I learned while growing up was taught to me with actions more than words. My family never missed a Sunday at church. We ate every evening meal and Sunday dinner together. We stayed at the table until everyone was finished. By example, I learned how to prioritize faith, family, and other things.

    For balance, you first need a foundation. Then, you need practice. Coaching is the same. The more you coach with balance the better you get at it. If you are an unbalanced coach, you will not coach for long. Either you or others will become dissatisfied with your work and you will either quit or be let go.

    People admire others who have longevity in their professions. In the basketball coaching world, names like John Wooden, Dean Smith, Pat Summitt, Mike Krzyzewski, Bobby Knight, Jim Boeheim, Muffet McGraw, Tom Izzo, Denny Crum, and the late Kay Yow come to mind. They could not have stayed "on the beam" for so long without great balance.

Maintaining balanced relationships with your family, players, and parents is challenging for a coach. Your family has to come before the players and their parents. I stopped coaching a varsity team after five years when my son was three years old because I had a real conflict of interests. He was in bed in the morning when I left to teach and in bed when I returned from coaching in the evening.

Does it make me right and others wrong? Absolutely not! Circumstances may be the same but each coach will prioritize those circumstances differently. Some parents work and use child care; others don't. Both can be successful.

I returned to the same basketball program at the same school and coached in five different decades. Each stint was different. The difference in my age and the players was obvious, but the ball, the rim height, and the fundamentals were the same. Most importantly, my balance was still good.

Player relationships are always key to balanced coaching. A coach has a relationship with every player she coaches. If each player-coach relationship is balanced between being a coach and a confidant, the overall result will be successful. A twenty-year-old athlete will not come to a coach's office to talk about his father's serious illness, cry, and open his heart if there is not a balanced relationship. The player will go elsewhere. Sometimes a student athlete will tell her college coach she is getting engaged before she tells her parents.

My point is that a student athlete will come to a coach for help or to share if they have a respectful balanced relationship. This relationship did not develop overnight or by correcting footwork on a jump shot. This coach-player relationship was built over time, off the court and on. The coach was on that balance beam, teetering from side to side at times, trying to form the relationship. Why? Because if a player has a strong and balanced relationship with her coach, the athlete will accept coaching more enthusiastically. Without it, the coach is just one more authority figure telling her what to do.

A coach once told me he needed to earn the right to coach a player. He needed to form a firm relationship with his players before he could really coach them on the court. The players would then know it was coaching and not a personal attack when the coach instructed them.

Some coaches say, "I don't want to be a player's friend. I want that separation between coach and player." Again, every coach will deal with the same circumstances differently. A coach's success and longevity tells a lot about the coach. Men and women who coach for a lifetime will have player-coach relationships that last forever.

Although the balancing of family and player-coach relationships is important, all of the other issues that cause a coach to lose his balance are also crucial. Parents, community, the school administration and colleague relationships are paramount if you are to stay on the path to coaching success.

What determines success at the end of the year or at the end of a coaching career? What can a coach do to get a 10 on the balance beam? (Most of us would settle for a 7 or 8 because of all the factors that play into the score.) The answer is easy. Every coach should be going into coaching to make a difference for the better. Every player you coach, every parent, fan, and colleague will hopefully be better for what you did. And, you will be better for everything they did.

That might sound unrealistic but in many cases it is the norm. I am not saying leaders live in a perfect world where the score on every apparatus will be a 10. It is, however, what they should strive for. Perfection may never be attained by any of us, but we continue to try.

The coach can see the success of many without being told. There are also times when situations could have gone better. Hopefully, all parties learned from it and became better for it.

For example, I had to ask a very hard question of a senior player. A "reliable" source had seen him smoking. I asked the question and told him the consequences before he answered. He looked me straight in the eye and said, "You didn't coach me to be a liar; so, yes, I was smoking." He left the team. Eventually he became the owner of two successful businesses and we are the best of friends to this day.

Many coaching friends of mine have had players with little or no financial means. Socks, basketball shoes, and things other kids take for granted were never theirs. These coaches made sure these players were taken care of discreetly. And, many of the recipients returned to thank their coach's years later.

Every coach has stories about those they have helped. The difficult, maybe more meaningful, ones don't get discussed as often. It is safe to say that in these cases the coaches made a difference.

Recently, I was blessed to be in a situation that brought the balance in coaching together. It was an unbelievable experience. I was at a high school basketball game, recruiting a player for the college. As I stood by the door to the gym, deciding where I would sit, I noticed a familiar person standing next to me. It was a referee who had worked many of the high school games I coached years ago. We sat down together.

Shortly thereafter, a young man walked into the gym. The referee recognized him as an athletic director who had often hired him. To my surprise, I realized I had coached this same young man when he was a twelve-year-old little league baseball player. I had not seen him for at least twenty-two years. He sat down and joined us.

At halftime, I went to the popcorn stand. As I was turning to go back into the gym, a man looked at me like he knew me. I did not recognize him. He said my name and I was at a loss for his. He told me his name and said that he had coached at the school we were at that night some fifty years ago. He remembered coaching against me when I was a player at Rockford High School.

The balancing act was complete. We have a player to start a new relationship with, a referee friend, a former player and friend, a coach that remembered me, and me. Twenty-two years to fifty years separated the space of time since we had seen each other under one circumstance or another. We spoke to each other as if no time had passed. The floor was now balanced with each of these people being placed in my path that night.

Coaching is about balance. It is about holding yourself accountable to that balance in order to be successful.

If you waver too far, one way or the other, you will need to self-correct or you will fall. My mother told me that athletics is very much like life: you have to come back time and time again. Put more simply, if you fall, get up. Your balance will hopefully return.

The first goal in coaching should be to create an atmosphere in which a group can thrive successfully.

You don't have to be a chemist to coach, but you do have to be good at chemistry if you want to be a successful coach.

Chapter 4
Chemistry

Simply speaking, chemistry comes down to making sense out of a lot of different parts, researching many facts, making hypotheses, and coming to solutions. If you look at something underneath a microscope, it is magnified so that you can take a close look at it. Sometimes the object(s) are still and sometimes they are moving. Whichever the case may be, you will have a better picture in your eye and can now move forward with some conclusions.

Athletic coaches take this approach as they view players individually practicing their jump shots, ball handling, or jumping rope. They also see players moving together as they practice as a team. It is all about making sense out of a lot of different things.

Chemistry to a coach can take on many forms. The five basketball players on the floor must act together and that takes five minds working as one. If the players are not in sync with each other, the obvious will happen. Sub ☺! Different combinations of players will produce different results.

As a coach places players under the microscope, they are researching what combinations will give the team the best chemistry. It takes a considerable amount of time to draw conclusions from DNA samples or molecules in a chemistry laboratory. The same is true in finding the players that have the best TEAM chemistry or which players perform the best together in a particular unit.

The success or failure on the playing field or court will be reached faster, and at a higher level, when the player to player and coach to player relationship is genuinely effective.

A coach's relationship with his athletes and team plays a tremendous part in the group's success or lack of it. That is such an obvious statement you might find it to be an oversimplification. However, do you know any coach who has had chemistry issues when it comes to players, parents, staff, or the administration? I'm sure you know of at least one who may have become so discouraged with his relationships that he gave up coaching.

The chemistry between a player and her coach can be very, very strong. And, that bond is something only a coach and the player can describe because it is different in each coach-player situation.

It was pointed out at a coaching clinic that young people look to their parents as role models about 65% of the time. The next closest role models are coaches at 6%, followed by church clergy at 3%. That is a lot of responsibility for a coach!

Chemistry within a team is not something that automatically produces a winning season, but without it the view under the microscope can be distorted and difficult to adjust. Good chemistry starts with one relationship at a time and spreads throughout the team. When it carries over to all of the players on the team, it is truly a beautiful thing to observe. Chemistry magnifies itself to such a point that the bond, the DNA, of the group becomes so strong it is difficult for teams with lesser chemistry to beat them.

Most basketball coaches are aware of Coach John Wooden's Pyramid of Success. The "Pyramid of Success" is built on what Coach Wooden views as the cornerstones to success and in between the cornerstones are five base parts that unite it together; Industriousness, Friendship, Loyalty, Cooperation, and Enthusiasm.

The Pyramid has levels; at the top is Success. Every block in the Pyramid is essential to building your own success. If you adhere to the Pyramid, your chances of being successful are very good. Ambition, Adaptability, Resourcefulness, Fight, Faith, Patience, Reliability, Integrity, Honesty, and Sincerity are some of the areas Coach Wooden sees as esential to becoming a successful person.[1]

"Only one person can judge it—you. You can fool everyone else, but in the final analysis only you know whether you goofed off or not."[2]

"Success is peace of mind which is a direct result of

---

[1]　　John Wooden with Jack Tobin. They Call Me Coach (New York: McGraw-Hill, 2004). 85-86.
[2]　　Ibid. 85-86.

self-satisfaction in knowing you did your best to become the best you are capable of becoming."[3]

One could quote John Wooden often and not repeat. He is not only a great coach but a true philosopher.

If a coach shares the teachings of John Wooden's Pyramid with her team, the chemistry desired will be created because everyone wants to be successful as an individual and as a team.

The first goal in coaching should be to create an atmosphere in which a group can thrive successfully.

One way players see chemistry is by observing the coaching staff. It quickly becomes evident to a player if the head coach and his assistants support each other, want to work together, and are moving in the same direction for the benefit of the team. Assistant coaches who have their own agendas are not a benefit to any coaching staff.

Another example of group chemistry is to watch a flock of geese fly. This is literally an example of chemistry in motion.

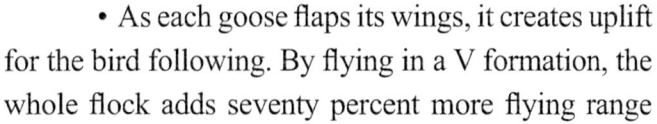

o———————o

• As each goose flaps its wings, it creates uplift for the bird following. By flying in a V formation, the whole flock adds seventy percent more flying range than if each bird flew alone.

---
3   *Ibid. 88-89.*

Lesson: People who share a common direction and sense of community can get where they are going quicker and easier because they are traveling on the thrust of one another.

o———————o

• When a goose falls out of formation, it suddenly feels the drag and resistance of trying to fly alone and quickly gets back into formation to take advantage of the lifting power of the birds immediately in front.

Lesson: If we have as much sense as a goose, we will join the formations of those who are headed where we want to go.

o———————o

• When the lead goose gets tired, it rotates back into the formation and another goose flies at the point position.

Lesson: It pays to take turns doing the hard tasks of sharing leadership.

o———————o

• The geese in formation honk from behind to encourage those up front to keep up their speed.

Lesson: We need to make sure our honking from behind is encouraging—not something unhelpful.

o———————o

• When a goose gets sick, wounded, or is shot down, two geese drop out of formation and follow it down to help provide protection. They stay with this member until they are able to fly again, when they launch out on their own to find another formation or start their own flock.

Lesson: If we have as much sense as geese, we'll stand by one another.[4]

○─────────○

I shared this story with a ninth-grade girl's basketball team that had not won a game as seventh or eighth graders. To say they took the story to heart would be an understatement. They came out in a V formation and honking to start their pre-game warm-up. Their parents had to honk at another player if they passed them in a car and their t-shirts had geese on them. They went 16-4. ☺

These girls are now college age and still talk about THE season. They see geese in the sky and remember learning about team chemistry and how it still applies today. Coaches who can create this type of chemistry are going to win. They may not win all their games, but they will win players and be able to teach them life skills that will help them be productive citizens.

You can read other books for examples of chemistry and how it applies to the game and to life. These examples show how we should do things if we are part of a group moving in the same direction. Remember, parts of something are just that—parts. It is the whole that makes the difference. If you turn the M in me upside down you obviously have WE.

4 Reprinted from Ann Lander's column; date and author unknown

Team chemistry consists of individual parts: the coaches, the players, the manager, the statisticians, and many others. Success will come if cornerstones are laid as a foundation; building blocks are added to the pyramid; and the team, as individuals and as a group, climb to the top together.

It is all about coming together with a common purpose and trying to become as closely bonded as possible. The individuals may not have the same DNA but the group very likely will be close.

A coach's chemistry lab is the athletic field or court where she performs research, forms hypotheses, and come to conclusions from her investigations every day. She publishes articles on her conclusions to share her findings so others can move forward with additional research.

All vocations are needed to instruct young people with life skills. Industriousness, cooperation, enthusiasm, loyalty, friendship, ambition, honesty, integrity, resourcefulness, patience, and faith are some of the tools that every person needs to learn in one lab or another.

You don't have to be a chemist to coach, but you do have to be good at chemistry if you want to be a successful coach.

When you hear geese honking overhead, look up and be reminded of the teamwork necessary to be successful. Only you know if your team has it.

Building meaningful relationships with players, parents, fans, and administration will help you attain longevity in the coaching profession.

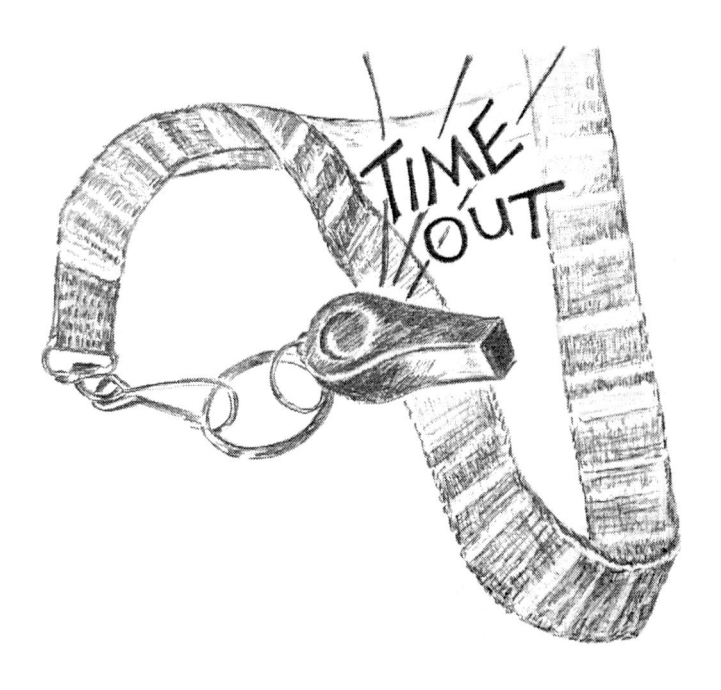

Coaches choose to work with people because they want to make a positive difference.

Chapter 5
Perspective

It is important to keep things in perspective. According to Random House Webster's College Dictionary, perspective means "one's mental view of facts, ideas, etc." (fifth definition) or "the ability to see all the relevant data in a meaningful relationship" (sixth definition). Because there are so many things for coaches to keep in perspective, this chapter is broken into four parts.

1. The Facts

How do successful coaches keep things in perspective in spite of the challenges and opportunities they face every day? What are the relevant data a coach considers? The easy answer is to keep things in balance, prioritize, and learn how to juggle. The more difficult question is how do coaches keep perspective for specific situations?

Coaches work with young people of varying ages and both genders. Each student brings a unique set of "DNA" to the team. Thus, coaches work to address each player in ways as to bring the entire group to a cohesive unit.

When choosing a coaching staff, assistants, or a team, a coach needs to address the relationship issues with each person he is considering. It is understandable that the person doing the choosing will be attracted to experienced candidates. If the candidate, coach or player, is obviously going to be a chemistry problem, the selector would be wise to keep the "whole" in perspective to the "parts."

If the coaching staff, or team, is going to reach its maximum potential, they must all share the same perspective. Each must accept his or her role as it applies to the whole and contribute to the total effort with all he or she can give. If an individual wavers from the overall team goals and objectives, he or she will harm the effort of the group.

Many assistant coaches want to become head coaches. I wanted assistants to offer suggestions and to feel comfortable in their role. However, from time to time, an overzealous assistant coach can undermine the overall effort for their personal benefit.

If a player or assistant coach strays from their intended role, he or she will need to return to the flock or they will be a drag on the team. Simply stated, they need to get on board or get off the train. No successful team effort can afford to have dead weight deterring its progress. When and if, they become head coaches they can lead.

The great basketball coach Dean Smith of

The University of North Carolina described a coach as "a carriage pulled by a team of horses taking its passengers from one point to another" (paraphrased). He pointed out that the passengers would need to want to go where the coach was going or eventually there would be directional issues.

For example, if you have musicians who are not on the same page as the conductor, the end result will not be harmonious. The entire orchestra, including the conductor, must be in sync and have the same goals and objectives. It sounds so elementary; yet we all know how much work goes into a symphony performance or an athletic contest. Success or failure depends on the collective effort of the group.

What perspective should be expected from the coach? How should a coach proceed as a leader? Should a coach demand perfection or settle for whatever the group can achieve? Does a coach set goals low enough so that he knows the team will achieve them and therefore be "successful?" Or does he set realistic goals and aim for those?

How do you prioritize goals and measure them? Are you keeping things in perspective if the bar is too low, too high, or in between?

Coaches meet with their teams each year to set goals. Some examples of goals are: win every home game, win every game, win the league title, win the state championship, and be in better shape than every other team. What perspective should prevail? If the relevant data (facts, ideas) show there is a meaningful relationship among all of the parties involved, then anything may be possible.

The coach can *assist* her team by keeping things in perspective. Listening, offering suggestions, and keeping all lines of communication open between herself and the players, as well as player to player, are key.

The important word is *assist*. A coach should not limit a player's perspective. The coach is there to guide, direct, and keep things in perspective. A coach can harm a team's success if she limits the group's thinking. She can also harm a successful outcome if she doesn't encourage players to dream and to think they can achieve more success than they might realize.

Keeping goals in perspective is a difficult task! Leaders face the issue of whether to set the bar at lofty, possibly unattainable, goals or at goals that are lower but realistic. This begs the question: is it better to set attainable goals and then over-achieve or visa-versa?

Many coaches keep their teams' perspective toward success clear by setting short-term goals. A specific time frame is set to revisit these goals and to determine achievement or the lack of it. The initial goals are then kept, changed, or reworked in some way. The team, its relationships, its success, and all relevant data are put under the microscope again and refocused.

Some coaches break down a team's season into parts. Some treat scrimmages, non-conference games, conference games, and tournament games as segments. Others break the schedule into smaller pieces to be able to re-evaluate issues more often. This may be helpful in keeping things in perspective.

2. Winning and Losing

It is difficult to keep winning and losing in perspective. Players, coaches, parents, fans, and the administration all want to win every game every year. It simply does not happen often.

I was privileged as a coach to be part of two high school teams with undefeated regular season records. One boy's team and one girl's team. Our college team also went undefeated during a regular season. When it happens, it is rewarding for everyone. It is a rare accomplishment. Chemistry played a big part each time.

It is difficult to keep winning and losing in perspective when the bar is set so high. Is it wrong to have the perspective that you are going to win every game because you have won in the past?

Those of you who have achieved "perfection" know that it can be harmful to a point. Future expectations may not be met, which leads to disappointment and possible unrest. The team that won a conference title one year and finishes with a five hundred record the next year is viewed poorly by many. Did the coach really forget everything he knew in one year? ☺ Of course not.

Teams that follow are expected to perform at the same level, or close to it. It can encourage players to over-achieve in order to attain the previous team's accomplishments. It can also deter future teams from achieving reachable goals because they are under such a powerful microscope.

So, how is winning and losing kept in perspective? It depends on the ability of the people involved to view the facts and their capability to see the relevant data in a meaningful way. Sometimes it happens and sometimes it doesn't, and a great deal depends on the coach. As far as the coach is concerned, he can only control what he can control himself. What he says and does will be scrutinized by everyone involved.

And, it isn't so much what a coach says at the moment that matters the most, but rather what he did and said previously to establish valuable relationships with players, parents, fans, and the administration. The development of trust and understanding is important to keep things in perspective. That is the key. I have seen coaches who weather storms and not miss a beat after a sub-par season. I have also seen coaches come under unwarranted criticism just because they did not establish lasting relationships with ALL facets of the equation.

A coach, in my opinion, cannot just be a great x and o person.

Building meaningful relationships with players, parents, fans, and administration will help you attain longevity in the coaching profession.

The key word is meaningful. Coaches don't have to be best friends, buddies, or confidants with everyone. They do, however, need to gain people's trust, respect, and confidence. The above pertains to all professions.

Can you be a successful coach and not be great at the x's and o's? Absolutely! Let's review: if you have good players you will usually win; if you don't, you won't. Therefore, it is possible for a coach to be successful but he will not have longevity unless he learns the game. Winning covers up many things, but sooner or later the truth will be known.

3. Opinions

As I recruit high school basketball players for our college team, I visit public and parochial schools in many states and of all sizes. I visit some schools with excellent coaches who have done the necessary things to help their following keep winning and losing in perspective.

I hear parents, fans, and administrators voice their opinions about the high school athletes. It is my pleasure to report that more times than not they keep things in perspective. Really! I was surprised.

Sometimes I just listen to the local banter about the team and sometimes I engage in conversation. Parents will say things like "the team was not very strong this year" or "the team is great this year, which is unusual." Fans will say "they appreciate the team's effort" and "they support the team whether they win or lose."

It almost sounds too good.

I also hear negative comments, but usually they are limited and typically occur when the team is losing. Four comments are consistent: "The referees are not calling anything," "why don't the referees let them play," "the popcorn is too salty tonight," or "why don't they salt the popcorn?" I love recruiting almost as much as coaching!

A parent's perspective is unique. I can address this topic from a parent's viewpoint and as a coach. As a parent of three children, two boys and a girl, who all played high school athletics, I have found it is a difficult task to keep the team, my child, and the coach in perspective.

I encourage parents of young children to have their kids go out for sports like swimming, golf, wrestling, track, or tennis. ☺ These are sports that do not require coaches to make as many judgment calls as in basketball, volleyball, or football. The head-to-head competition takes care of who is the fastest or best.

These coaches, however, still need to hold themselves accountable for teaching life skills but most of the playing time decisions are made for them by the athletes. Even though individual sports are still "team" sports, parents, fans, and fellow players can't disagree with a stopwatch or who just pinned whom.

Parents usually think their child is better than they are no matter what the activity. It takes a dedicated coach to build a parent-coach relationship that gets the parents on the same page or at least in the same chapter. I have seen it done over and over by good coaches. It takes time, thought, and energy to build that necessary trust.

Participation in school extra curricular activities like band, orchestra, a play, choir or an athletic team are not required as part of the curriculum. A student decides to join an activity, with parent permission, to be part of something they enjoy and hopefully can contribute to.

The parent is allowing their child to be led

and coached by someone other than themselves. With this decision by the student and the parent, it is important to give the leader-coach permission to make rules and hold members of the group accountable for their actions. The leader-coach needs to respect this opportunity and challenge by using appropriate techniques and behavior with each person in the group and be held accountable for their actions also.

The leader wants the student to come to them first with individual questions or group problems. This is not intended to avoid a parent but to allow the student to experience the life skill of talking to the person in charge to discuss and solve a situation. It is not easy for most people to take questions or issues to a person of authority. This is an opportunity for a young person to learn a valuable life skill.

The parent-leader relationship is so important when their child has a problem within a group or with the leader. This relationship is not cultivated by just the wave of a hand to say hi, an email or a message carried to or from the parent or leader. It takes a concentrated and committed effort by both the leader and the parent to make this relationship a positive one. Both parties want the student to have a great experience in the activity and communication is essential to accomplish this.

It all boils down to trust!

The leader must explain to the group and the parent the appropriate action for the student to take if a problem arises. A parent will not need to contact the school principal or the athletic director before the student and leader have had adequate time to come to an understanding if all three parties trust the process and allow it to take its course. Long hard practices and events held over a vacation time are typical examples of possible misunderstandings. Playing time in certain sports is a classic issue.

Parents should inform proper school personnel about illegal activity or inappropriate behavior by a leader-coach. School personnel must contact a parent if a student is involved in an illegal activity or uses inappropriate behavior also. Athletic training rules also hold a student to an additional set of regulations

There are also parents who are very happy their child made the team. They "get it." They understand and enjoy what their child is receiving from being on a team that is coached by a person teaching sport and life skills. They are usually the parents who have the team over for spaghetti dinners. ☺ For all the right reasons, of course. My wife prepared more spaghetti dinners for the teams than I would like to count. It helped the team chemistry to do something together away from the court.

I have had numerous parents thank me for

"letting" their child be on the team. My answer to them is always that I didn't let their child make the team. They made it because they deserved it. But I always thank them and usually am able to say that their child is an asset to the team and it is a reflection of their parenting.

In my opinon the following are true in sports and any other art form:

1. If you have good players you usually win; if you don't, you won't.

2. Poor shooters, mediocre soloists and average musicians are always available.

3. Parents usually think their children are better than they really are.

4. You will receive more from coaching than you give.

It is not the right of every student to be on an athletic team, play first chair in the band or sing a solo in the choir. It is a privilege to make the cut. It is the result of a person spending a lot of time practicing, making a concentrated effort, and having the correct attitude. The coach keeps everything in perspective as she chooses the team or an individual for a task.

4. Life-Long Influence

To bring the whole coaching perspective full circle, ask yourself what coaches impacted you the most and why. Is there a coach from your past with whom you keep in touch because he or she is still important to you? If yes, write down what he or she did or said that has remained with you.

Maybe a coach motivated you and your teammates in a special way. Maybe that coach is the reason you are coaching today or your coaching style mimics theirs. Maybe that coach had such an impact on your life that you continue to thank him or her to this very day. Maybe that coach was your role model because of the way they taught sports and life skills.

Scott Hedman, former head coach of the Kansas City Knights, wrote the following about the lasting effect his former coach, Cotton Fitzsimmons, had on him. "I believe we all felt important to Cotton because he was so important to us. This was Cotton's gift. He was able to tailor each relationship he had with each player to that player's personality, strengths and weaknesses. If a player needed a father figure, a best friend, a coach to crack the whip—whatever the need—Cotton was there" [5]

My junior high basketball coach is the reason I became a coach. I loved the game of basket-

---
[5] *Chicken Soup for the Soul: Inside Basketball (Chicken Soup for the Soul Publishing, LLC, 2009), page 253*

ball from the first time I touched the ball, but it was this coach who became my role model. He was firm, treated every player with respect, and knew the game well. He had the team's respect because of how he taught us the game and how he taught us life skills.

He always came to practice in typical coaching gear but he was a person who carried himself in a way that we would do anything for him. He commanded our attention due to his demeanor and he never had to demand anything from his players. We wanted to please him. We were seventh and eighth graders yet he treated us like we were the high school varsity team.

Evidence of Coach's perspective of a team and its players was shown in an article that was printed in the local newspaper at the end of our eighth-grade season. We had just completed an undefeated season and won a three-game tournament against very good teams. We won all three tournament games by two points and every game had its highlights and contributions from key players. We were huge underdogs in the championship game. Our team had to come from behind to win.

The reporter talked about how our team played unselfishly all year and due to that type of effort we had been victorious. Our unbeaten record was attributed to the team's ability to play together and have a good attitude.

Anyone reading the article had to note that not one player's name was mentioned—names were only listed underneath the team photo. There was no mention of the leading scorer or re-bounder. There was no mention of key plays or any individual performances.

We were proud of our coach and proud to be on his team.

Years later, when I was coaching women's college basketball, Coach made a point to come to some of our games. He surprises me when I see him there. It is a compliment to have him make that effort. He comes for me, but I hope he realizes his mentoring has evolved into something he can be proud of.

I have told him many times of his impact on me and my coaching. He humbly thanks me and acts like he was just doing his job. Yes, he was doing his job, but, in my opinion, he was doing his job the only way it should be done. He kept teaching sport skills and life skills in perspective.

Coach made me a better basketball player and developed my skills. He also shared the love of sport and specifically the game of basketball. More importantly, he made me a better person. No person has had an impact on my life as much as my junior-high basketball coach other than my parents.

A poem written for UCLA coach John Wooden by one of his former players, Swen Nater, describes my junior high coach perfectly.

I saw love once. I saw it clear
It had no leash. It had no fear.
It gave itself without a thought.
No reservation had it bought.
It seemed so free to demonstrate.
It seemed obsessed to orchestrate.
A symphony, designed to feed,
Composed to lift, the one in need.
Concern for others was its goal.
No matter what would be the toll.
It's strange just how much care it stores
To recognize its neighbor's sores.
And doesn't rest until the day
It's helped to take the sores away.
The joy retains and does not run
Until the blessing's job is done.
I saw love once, 'Twas not pretend.
He was my coach.
He is my friend.

Coaches choose to work with people because they want to make a positive difference.

It takes a special person to keep the relevant data in perspective, to develop meaningful relationships, and to lead a group successfully.

In a perfect world, players would play, coaches would coach, referees would referee, parents would be parents, administrators would administrate, and fans would cheer.

Coaches know they do not live in a perfect world. But neither do the other people involved in the activity or sport they are leading. Coaches can only try to be an example and teach the life skill of cooperation which will help prepare players for the future.

Don't measure your coaching success by whether or not you receive supportive letters, emails, and phone calls or win all of your games. Just know that during your career you can touch thousands of lives in a positive way and that you have kept the many facets of coaching in perspective.

Balance and perspective allow you to handle stress in a good way.

Chapter 6
Good Stress

Choosing to become a coach entails responsibility in many forms. Decisions must be made. Some need to be made quickly; some after long-term planning. Some decisions are magnified by the moment or by the situation. Regardless of the time frame or specific crisis, decisions need to be made and carried out by the leader.

The outcome of a situation will more likely be positive if the leader has experience dealing with it. When my dad taught me to ride a two-wheeler, he knew from the experience of teaching my sister that I would probably fall a few times. Therefore, he was ready and knew what tactics to apply to keep me upright.

The inexperienced coach will be placed in situations he or she did not know existed. No matter how well prepared a coach is, there are new issues that will come up. Hopefully, as experiences accumulate, you will improve the way you handle situations and become even a better leader.

This is where the distress begins for most coaches. We are out of our comfort zone and need to make a decision. If a quick move has to be made, we don't have time to ask a more experienced co-worker or to Google it. We can only draw on our best personal resources and hope to solve the issue.

Some coaches panic. Some coaches remain calm. Some either avoid or run from unpleasant situations. Others embrace challenges. Your reaction is usually based on your past more than it is on the current issue. All of your personal experiences, good and bad, will assist you in handling the current situation.

Stress is what you make of it. Some people respond better under pressure than others. Why? I think mostly because they may have had more stress in their lives and have learned how to deal with situations calmly. I prefer to think of stress as something we all deal with and like muscles in your body; the more you use it the better we are at keeping it in perspective.

The ability to calm oneself, or stay calm, is instilled in some and not in others. Athletes who step up to the line and hit free throws in stressful situations may handle stress in a work situation better than those who have not had that or a similar experience.

If I had any success in coaching it was because I was able to stay calm under pressure. Even when I was not calm, I appeared calm. I stated in an earlier chapter there is probably a musician in every coach. I think there is an actor in every leader as well.

Sometimes it isn't how smart you are but how others perceive you to be. I'm sure you can think of times when you had to make quick decisions and weren't sure you were right. Every player thought you knew what you were doing, and trusted your lead.

I was able to get through many stressful situations by acting calm, knowledgeable, decisive and like I'd been there a million times. Most of you know exactly what I mean. Coaches draw on the best resources we have and present them in such a way that others follow.

In timeouts I would look straight into players' eyes and ask the five in the game if their heads were clear and if they were ready to take direction. If there was hesitation, I substituted. They needed to learn to stay in the now and to focus. Hopefully that was a life skill lesson.

One of my biggest compliments in this area came from a doctor. My son had fallen fifteen feet through the hay hatch in our barn and landed on cement. He was unconscious at my feet. When we arrived at the emergency room, they transported him to Hackley Hospital in Muskegon. He was unconscious for two days. Miraculously, he had no ill effects other than the swelling in his brain that caused him to stay unconscious. When I saw the emergency room doctor some time later, he said he had never seen anyone remain so calm when their four-year-old son was in such danger. He said my composure allowed him and his staff to do their jobs.

To say coaches offer to lead because they enjoy stress would be going too far. They do enjoy the preparation, the team building, the relationship building, and the games. In my opinion, and not to over simplify, I think there is good stress and bad stress.

When good stress becomes bad stress it may be time to stop and refocus. Are you, as a coach and leader, in balance? Are you keeping things in perspective? Do you have your priorities straight with who you are and who you want to be? Do you have a conflict of interest with what you are doing?

Balance and perspective allow you to handle stress in a good way.

I prefer to think of stress as challenges and opportunities; not as a bad thing. Keep your focus on working with individuals for the group good, teaching them life skills as well as sport skills, and helping young people mature into productive citizens and generally being a positive role model. This perspective will help you move forward with hope in your coaching career.

When all seems to not be going well and bad

stress begins to build, you need to have a plan in place to handle it. Talking to another coach who understands your situation can be helpful. Ask others you respect for advice. Read something of a positive nature. Most importantly, confront the problem and don't let it grow out of proportion.

Not everyone is meant to lead or coach. If you measure success only by wins and losses you are missing the whole point. A group can have success in many ways. Just because the flutist plays a wrong note or a player makes a bad pass doesn't mean the total project is lost.

If good relationships are established, solid coaching techniques are used, and if you handle the stressful situations as opportunities and challenges, you will be successful.

Just remember, winning games is not the only winning you can accomplish. The hearts and minds of the young people you coach will challenge you to be balanced, stay in perspective, and mindful of building relationships.

What a great opportunity you have as a coach!

We are out of timeouts!
*A coaching/leadership position is filled
with opportunities and challenges.
Try to stay in the "Right Lane" while you are
"Coaching at Seventy Miles Per Hour".*

Chapter 7
Personal Rewards

Obviously I love to coach and have been doing it off and on (more on than off) for a significant period of time. I have tried my best to honor my priorities of faith, family, and all the other stuff. Sometimes I had to check my balance because of the time associated with coaching, but for the most part it has been good.

My father and mother were the most balanced people I ever knew. They supported my activities which included sports, band, choir, and church. They never talked to a coach about anything. They kept everything in perspective.

I think my dad pumped out his chest more when I conquered the two-wheeler than when I received All Conference in basketball. I know my mother was proudest of me when I graduated from college.

I have tried to coach my children as I was coached by my parents. I am very blessed with the results. The biggest difference has been that my parents were not athletes and I was. This brings home the point that coaching comes in many different forms.

I hope you have a wonderful and rewarding coaching experience.

The following are excerpts of letters I have received from friends, colleagues, players, and family. They are evidence that I have received far more from coaching than I could ever give.

"The guys on the 1965-66 basketball team had been looking forward to that year since grade school; we were all related or buddies. I appreciated his passion and knowledge of the game, his sense of humor, his kindness and his challenging us as players. During our first game of the year, the other coach calls a timeout. He spends the first half of the timeout explaining why their coach called timeout, the adjustment the OTHER coach was going to make. And then told us what we needed to do. I remember smiling to myself and knowing then it was going to be a great year"
Bill

"You had a lasting impact on me and my career as a teacher and coach. My years under your guidance were very productive and rewarding. So, I thank you again for just being you. A man who has always had high standards, integrity, faith and a servant's spirit. Thanks again coach."
Bob

"In writing this letter, it is difficult not to be overwhelmed by a flood of memories, which go all the way back to my 8th grade year & In the intervening forty-two years, I have been your student, player, client, husband of one of your teachers, teacher to your children, parent of one of your players and, always and forever, a friend."

Barney

"I have many good memories from high school, several of which come from time spent as one of your tennis players. Perhaps my most memorable moment, the moment when I realized that I was so incredibly fortunate to have such a wonderful coach, was my freshman year during the finals at Regionals. When I could not get it together and compose myself, you would not give up on me. I remember you drawing on the back of a manila envelope a step-by-step plan of what I needed to do. It worked. You guided me to success in much the same way over the next four years."

Marta

"As our varsity basketball coach, Dean was my first mentor. He was the one that gave me the chance to coach at the high school level and I will never forget that. He cared about every athlete that he coached and went out of his way to get to know

them, not just coach them. He would always come in and talk to the kids about how to be successful on and off the court. That is always one of the important lessons he always taught the people around him, whether it be his athletes, boys at summer camp or his assistant coaches: how to be successful off the court. It is staggering when I think about the number of people I meet who have in one way or another been taught or coached by Dean. I am lucky to have had the chance to coach under him."
    Pete

    "There is so much you have taught me. You are always willing to spend as much time with me as I need. You passed on the story of the geese that I will never forget. My basketball team had not previously won a game and they took the story to heart. They went 16-4. Without you those lessons would not have been learned. Whenever I run into a player/parent from that team, they always say it was the best year they had ever seen."
    Liz

    "I would like to join the many others in wishing you the very best in your retirement. For many years I have observed you both on and off the court of competition. You were a great opponent, a competitive gentleman and a role model to area coaches and area youth. I can say you are a family man, a man of integrity and a difference maker."
    Mike

"For a while now, I have been hearing rumors about you nearing retirement. More recently however, especially in the last 10 or 20 years, those rumors have become increasingly more frequent. As a journalist, I listen to rumors, I enjoy rumors, but I demand facts. Are you actually planning to retire or is this just one of those stories you and John Mooy have decided to circulate just for the fun of it? If you really are retiring, I wish you the best, and I pray that God will continue to bless you and your family."
Rich

"Through our mutual love for basketball, you taught us invaluable life lessons. We didn't realize it at the time but you were teaching us a life philosophy--do things the right way. You taught us to play basketball the right way and thereby encouraged us to be students the right way, husbands the right way, fathers the right way and to do our jobs the right way. Given the success many of us that played for you have been lucky enough to achieve, I think your message got though. Congratulations on retiring."
Tony

"Thanks for being a great dad. You always made time for us even if you were working. Work never got in the way of being at our games, recitals, etc. because we were your priority. Thanks for setting a great example of work ethic. You taught all of us to how to commit and work hard. You set a great example of being a Christian leader by serving others first."

Brian, your son

"Dad's passions are now my passions. I enjoy coaching others & helping them find the best in themselves by giving them direction and lifting them up. I love my kids and my wife. I am passionate about sports. Thank you for coaching me and for helping Brian and I with the MBBA (Michigan Barn Ball Association). I want to be able to influence my kids lives the way you did mine."

Jeff, your son

"People trust you and see you as someone who has their best interests at heart. I think the fact that you make people laugh speaks volumes. I think of you often when I am at work and I am doing something that amuses others. You have taught me to be confident in the profession I have chosen. I feel like I can do anything above and beyond what I am doing. Thanks for not retiring from being my dad. That is the job in your life that I think you are best at!!"

Emily, your daughter

Coach Since
-1962-

Guard
-1958-

"We didn't really know what to call coach D. Morehouse at first. Mr. Morehouse was definitely too formal and our headcoach, his son Brian, was already known as Coach Mo. Big Mo seemed to be the natural fit, but eventually we dropped the Mo and added a little "gie" to make it simply Biggie. Perfect. It is now used so often, I doubt many at Hope College know his real name."

Jodie (Boom) Smith
Former Hope College player (1998-2002)
Holland, Michigan

About the Author

Dean was raised on sports. As a boy growing up in Rockford, Michigan he and the neighbor kids played basketball in the driveway, football in a neighbor's back yard and organized North-South games. (Courtland Street was the dividing line).

As a teenager he helped Red Auerbach coach the Boston Celtics many times as he watched NBA basketball on the families black and white television set. He also paid very close attention to every move UCLA coach John Wooden made as the Bruin's won championships.

His favorite NBA team was the Boston Celtics because of their unselfish play. Bob Cousy was his favorite player because of his ball handling skills and Cous just made everybody on the Celtics better. John "Hondo" Havalchak became his favorite Celtic along with Bill Russell, Sam Jones and K.C. Jones.

Dean played one on one in the driveway with Earl "the Pearl" Monroe and the "Big O" Oscar Robertson only to lose by a basket each time.

His athletic, coaching and other experiences in high school and college, as well as his current activities, are outlined next. They are varied and the reason he uses music, art, theatre and athletics to make his point in the book about everyone being a coach.

Dean has been married for forty-five years. He and his wife have three children and six grandchildren.

• *Education*
Rockford Public Schools: K-12
Michigan State University: Undergraduate B.S. degree-History Major, Physical Education Minor
Western Michigan University: Graduate Masters Degree in Elementary Administration

• *Employment*
Fremont Public Schools: Teacher and coach from 1962-1978
Fremont Public Schools: Continued coaching until 2000
The White Insurance Agency: Agent and part owner from 1978-2005
Hope College: 2000 to present

• *High School Athletics*
Basketball-Four years
    First Team All Conference in 1958 (The Grand Valley Conference)
    Honorable Mention Class B All State in 1958
Tennis- Four years
    First Team All Conference in 1958
Football-Two years
Cross Country- Two years
Inducted into the Rockford Hall of Fame as an athlete in 2005

- *Music and Theatre*

High School Choir (tenor) and Church Choir
Barbershop Quartet- The Klef Kings placed first in the Great Lakes Junior Barbershop Quartet competition in 1957
High School Plays- Trapp Family Singers (The Sound of Music) and Taming of the Shrew (Shakespeare)
High School Band (cornet-second chair)
Director of his Phi Gamma Delta Fraternity Chorus in the All Fraternity Sing at M.S.U.-First place

- *Coaching*

Junior high football and junior varsity football
Boy's eighth grade and ninth grade basketball
Boy's junior varsity basketball, boy's varsity basketball and girl's varsity basketball as a volunteer assistant in 1977
Girl's varsity tennis and boy's varsity tennis
Started Fremont's summer tennis program in 1962
Regional Class B Tennis Coach of the Year in 1993
Region 4 Class B Basketball Coach of the Year in 1996-97
Hope College Women's Varsity Basketball Assistant from 2000 to present • D3 National Championship in 2006

- *Currently*

Church music program and various church boards
Fremont Tennis Association Board member
Fremont Lake Association Board member
Newaygo County Boy's and Girl's Club Board member
Fremont Rotary Club current member-Paul Harris Fellow

- *Other*

Fremont Area Community Foundation Board member for fourteen years
Co-founder of the Fremont High School National Honor Society- Steven S. Nisbet Chapter
Co-founder of the Michigan Barnball Association with his three children

YOUR COACHING GAME PLAN

I am currently doing this:
1. _____
2. _____
3. _____
4. _____
5. _____
6. _____
7. _____
8. _____
9. _____
10. _____

Possible changes or additions:
1. _____
2. _____
3. _____
4. _____
5. _____
6. _____
7. _____
8. _____
9. _____
10. _____

The book and CD will not be available in stores or online.

Dean H. Morehouse
6163 W. Lakeview Drive
Fremont, Michigan 49412
231-924-2092
dean.morehouse@gmail.com